D1092432

lessons from
NATURE
for youth

lessons from NATURE for youth

a reprint of an 1836 original

WallBuilder PRESS

Aledo, Texas

Lessons From Nature for Youth
Reprinted in 1995 by WallBuilders.
Second Edition, Second Printing, June 2003

Cover Design: Jeremiah Pent

For additional copies of this book, or for information on other
books and reprints, contact WallBuilders, PO Box 397, Aledo, TX
76008, 817-441-6044, www.wallbuilders.com.

Printed in the United States of America

ISBN 0-925279-46-3

CONTENTS.

FACT I.

THE YOUNG BISON.

The tenderest affection is due to a mother,   - Page 13

FACT II.

THE ANT.

What we fail to do at once may yet be accomplished, 14

FACT III.

THE GOLD-BREASTED TRUMPETER.

Good manners are becoming and graceful,   -   -   - 15

FACT IV.

THE GRASSHOPPER.

What is evil may be like what is good,   -   -   -   - 16

FACT V.

THE MONGREL.

Parents should be promptly and cheerfully obeyed, 18

FACT VI.

THE SWALLOW AND THE VULTURE.

All things have their use,   -   -   -   -   -   -   -   - 19

FACT VII.

THE GOAT SUCKER.

An evil name should never be given except it is deserved, - - - - - - - - - - - - - - 21

FACT VIII.

THE NEW ZEALANDERS.

People are to be esteemed, not according to the dress, but the mind, - - - - - - - - - 23

FACT IX.

THE MORA.

Avoid the beginning of evil, - - - - - - - - 25

FACT X.

DR. MURRAY AND MR. GIFFORD.

Important ends may be accomplished by humble means, but when it is practicable, the best should be employed, - - - - - - - - - - - 27

FACT XL

THE ISLAND WARRIORS.

Many are seriously injured by fright, - - - - - 29

FACT XII.

PETER THE GREAT, OBERLIN, AND RUPP.

Things declared to be impossible may be done, - - - 31

FACT XIII.

THE FIRE FLY.

Avoid all unkindness and cruelty, - - - - - - 33

FACT XIV.

THE MISSIONARIES' SERVANT.

Sound is often mistaken for sense, - - - - - - 35

FACT XV.

THE BEAVERS.

Union is strength, - - - - - - - - - - - 36

FACT XVI.

THE TURKEY COCK.

Mind your own business, - - - - - - - - - 38

FACT XVII.

THE WASPS.

Kindness may sometimes appear to be cruelty, - 39

FACT XVIII.

THE CHAMOIS HUNTER.

Danger should only be encountered when it is unavoidable, and to face it is praiseworthy, - - - 41

FACT XIX.

THE ESQUIMAUX.

Unfavourable circumstances have some alleviations, 44

FACT XX.

THE BEAR.

Parental affection is strong and tender, - - - - 46

FACT XXI.

THE HAWTHORN.

Strange tales are not always true, - - - - - - 48

FACT XXII.

THE ICHNEUMON.

Evil dispositions may break out, though for a time
concealed, - - - - - - - - - - - - - 51

FACT XXIII.

THE DESERT.

Common things are often undervalued, - - - - 53

FACT XXIV.

THE SLOTH.

Praise is often due where censure is given, - - - 55

FACT XXV.

THE LION.

Gratitude is delightful, but ingratitude is detestable, 60

FACT XXVI.

THE TRAVELLER.

The many should not be condemned for the errors
of the few, - - - - - - - - - - - - - 61

FACT XXVII.

THE BEDOUIN.

Prejudice against persons or things should be
avoided, - - - - - - - - - - - - - 62

FACT XXVIII.

THE KING OF THE VULTURES.

Superiors should be attended to before us, - - - 64

FACT XXIX.

THE ORCHIS.

That which is thought wrong may yet be right, - 64

FACT XXX.

THE THRUSHES.

All, but especially the suffering, should be treated
kindly - - - - - - - - - - - - - - 66

FACT XXXI.

THE CRIMEA.

Flattery injures the flatterer, - - - - - - - 68

FACT XXXII.

THE SECRETARY FALCON.

An innocent act may be thought vicious, - - - 69

FACT XXXIII.

THE FORAGERS.

Do unto others as ye would they should do unto
you, - - - - - - - - - - - - - - 70

FACT XXXIV.

TUPEE AND KORRO-KORRO.

Sincerity should be cherished, and hypocrisy abhorred, - - - - - - - - - - - - - 71

FACT XXXV.

THE MACAW.

Jealousy is disgraceful, - - - - - - - - - 73

FACT XXXVI.

THE ASSES OF THE ALPS.

" Let thine eyes look right on, and let thine eyelids look straight before thee," - - - - - - 74

FACT XXXVII.

THE CAMEL.

Anger is rarely wise, - - - - - - - - - - 76

FACT XXXVIII.

OBERLIN.

Contentment should be sought and cherished, - - 77

FACT XXXIX.

THE BULLFINCH.

It is only a good example that deserves imitation, 79

FACT XL.

THE PINNA AND ITS CANCER FRIEND.

A little aid may often be of great service, - - - 79

FACT XLI.

THE WOOD PECKER.

Truth is always precious, - - - - - - - - 81

FACT XLII.

THE ROOKS.

The sufferings of others should awaken sympathy, 83

FACT XLIII.

THE SPIDER, THE ANT LION, AND THE TREES.

Some see, but see not; while the knowledge of
others is greatly increased by observation, - - 85

FACT XLIV.

POMAREE.

Selfishness is vexatious, painful, and ruinous, - - 87

FACT XLV.

THE WHITE OWL.

All are dependent, - - - - - - - - - - - 89

FACT XLVI.

THE TORTOISE AND THE ELEPHANT.

Good feeling, though awkwardly expressed, is far
better than hypocritical courtesy, - - - - - 90

FACT XLVII.

THE MUSCLES.

When one means fails, try another, - - - - - 92

FACT XLVIII.

THE TURKS.

There is a right way and a wrong way, - - - - 92

FACT XLIX.

SNAKES AND MONKEYS.

Mischief is censurable, - - - - - - - - - 94

FACT L.

ABDOULRAHMAN.

The great are not always happy, - - - - - - 95

FACTS NOT FABLES.

I. THE YOUNG BISON.

The tenderest Affection is due to a Mother.

A SINGULAR and affecting trait is recorded of the bison, when young. Whenever a cow bison falls by the murderous hand of the hunters, and happens to have a calf, the helpless creature, instead of attempting to escape, stays by its fallen dam, with many expressions of strong affection. The mother being secured, the hunter makes no attempt on the calf, because this is unnecessary, but proceeds to cut up the carcass; and then, laying it on his horse, he returns home, followed by the young one, which thus instinctively accompanies the remains of its parent. A hunter once rode into the town of Cincinnati, between the Miames, followed in this manner by three calves, all of which had just lost their dams.

APPLICATION.

What feelings ought to be cherished in the bosom of a child toward a mother! Who can tell how much it owes her? Ah! it is far more than it can ever repay. Go then, my little reader, and kiss your mother; and tell her you will try to be good, and prove you are deeply sensible of her kindness and love! Perhaps she is ill;—how attentive, then, should you be to her, how quietly should you move about, that she may not be disturbed by noise; and how glad should you be to do any thing to assist or relieve her! But it may be she is a widow;—if so, she should be loved, if possible, still more tenderly. The undutiful children of a widowed mother are among the worst and most wicked of all.

II. THE ANT.

What we fail to do at once may yet be accomplished.

THE celebrated conqueror, Timour the Tartar, was once forced to take shelter from his enemies in a ruined building. There he sat alone for several hours. After some time, desirous of diverting his mind from his hope-

less condition, he fixed his attention on an
ant which was attempting to carry a grain
of corn, larger than itself, up a high wall. Its
efforts, however, were unsuccessful. Again
and again it strove to accomplish its object
—and failed. Still undaunted, it returned to
its task, and sixty-nine times did Timour see
the grain fall to the ground. But the *seven-
tieth* time the ant reached the top of the wall
with its prize; and "the sight," said the conqueror, who had just before been despairing,
"gave me courage at the moment, and I have
never forgotten the lesson it conveyed."

APPLICATION.

Nor should *we* forget it. We should first
see if a thing is *worth* doing, and if it be, and
we fail, we should try again and again, and
persevere until it is accomplished. If an ant
were not discouraged by sixty-nine failures,
when should a little boy or girl be disheartened?

III. THE GOLD-BREASTED TRUMPETER.

Good manners are becoming and graceful.

A GENTLEMAN, who had reared a gold-
breasted trumpeter, (a bird so called from the
wonderful noise it makes,) says,—"It treated
me with many marks of attention and regard:
when I opened its cage in the morning, the
kind animal hopped round me, expanding its
wings, and *trumpeting*, as if to wish me good

morning. He showed equal attention when I went out and returned. No sooner did he see me at a distance, than he ran to meet me; and even when I happened to be in a boat, and set my foot on shore, he welcomed me with the same compliments."

APPLICATION.

Some children hold their heads down, and creep along as if they had done something blamable, when they are about to meet persons whom they know. But this is very ill-behaved: relatives, friends, and acquaintances should always be treated with attention. A bow or a courtesy is easily made, and good manners are pleasing and delightful to those who have them, and to all who witness them.

IV. THE GRASSHOPPER.

What is Evil may be like what is Good.

"One afternoon," says Waterton, "not far from Monteiro, six or seven blackbirds, with a white spot between the shoulders, were making a noise, and passing to and fro on the lower branches of a tree in an abandoned, weed-grown, orange orchard. In the long grass underneath the tree, apparently a pale green grasshopper was fluttering, as though it had got entangled in it. When you once fancy that the thing you are looking at is really what you take it for, the more you

look at it, the more you are convinced it is
so. In the present case, this was a grasshopper beyond all doubt, and nothing more remained to be done but to wait in patience till
it had settled, in order that you might run no
risk of breaking its legs in attempting to lay
hold of it while it was fluttering—it still kept
fluttering; and having quietly approached it,
intending to make sure of it, behold, the head
of a large rattle snake appeared in the grass
close by : an instantaneous spring backward
prevented fatal consequences. What had
been taken for a grasshopper was, in fact,
the elevated rattle of the snake, in the act of
announcing that he was quite prepared, though
unwilling, to make a sure and deadly spring.
He shortly after passed slowly from under
the orange tree to the neighhouring wood on
the side of a hill; and as he moved over a
place bare of grass and weeds, he appeared
to be about eight feet long!"

MORAL.

Appearances are deceitful. Poisonous ber-
ries often look tempting—ice, when it sometimes seems sound, if ventured upon, will
break, and let him who is daring into the wa-
ters—and " wine when it giveth its colour in
the cup, at the last biteth like a serpent, and
stingeth like an adder." It was " when Eve
saw that the tree was pleasant to the eyes
that she took of the fruit thereof, and gave
also to her husband with her, and he did eat;"

and the issue was their being driven out from Eden, and all the misery that ever was, or will be endured. If then, a thing appears to be right, be sure it is so before you do it:— if a thing appears to be good, be sure it is so before you stretch out your hand to take it— or that which seemed to be a harmless grass-hopper, may prove a destructive rattle snake! And Zoroaster says, " When you doubt, abstain !"

V. THE MONGREL.

Parents should be promptly and cheerfully obeyed.

A MONGREL, that is, an animal between the shepherd's dog and terrier, a great favourite in a farm house, was standing by while his mistress was washing some of her children. On asking one she had just dressed to bring his sister's clothes from the next room, he pouted and hesitated.—"O then," said the mother, " Mungo will fetch them."

She thus spoke, it appears, by way of reproof and reproach : for he had not been accustomed, like many dogs, to fetch and carry. But Mungo was intelligent and obedient, and immediately brought the child's frock to his mistress.

APPLICATION.

Ah ! do not you blush, little boy ? Only a short time ago, when your mother told you to do something, you stood still and looked displeased. Nor was this the first instance of your disobedience; for you know you have done so again and again. And that little girl must not smile at your shame; she has been just as often in fault. Surely then you will both think of Mungo when you feel inclined to disobey, and not allow yourselves any more to be reproved by a dog!

———

VI. THE SWALLOW AND THE VULTURE.

All things have their use.

OF what *use* is that swallow? To this it may be replied, that swallows defend us, in a great measure, from the personal and domestic annoyance of flies and gnats, and, what is of more consequence, they keep down numbers of our little enemies, which, either in the grub or winged state, would otherwise prey on the husbandman's labours. Unproductive harvests are more frequent on the continent than in this country; and it is well known that swallows are caught and sold as food in the markets of Spain, France, and Italy. Doubtless, to this must be partly attributed a scarcity of corn.

Of what *use*, then, is a vulture? To those who have examined this bird, it appears evidently adapted to that share in the daily business of the world which has been allotted to it,—that of clearing away putrid matter, which might otherwise taint the air, and produce infectious disease.   And this it does in countries of great extent and thinly scattered population, principally by its extraordinary powers of *sight*.   In the year 1788, Mr. Baker, and several other gentlemen, were on a hunting party, in the island of Cossimbuzar, in Bengal.   They killed a wild hog of uncommon size, and left it on the ground near the tent.   An hour after, walking near the spot where it lay, the sky being perfectly clear, a dark spot in the air at a great distance attracted their attention. It appeared to increase in size, and move directly toward them : as it advanced it proved to be a vulture, flying in a direct line to the hog ; and in an hour, *seventy* others *came in all directions.*

APPLICATION.

Man often trifles, but God has made nothing in vain.   Every part of his works should excite our inquiry ; for it is capable of affording instruction.   Even creatures, commonly regarded as obnoxious, are useful, and to some of those which are deemed insignificant, or passed by with contempt, our obligation is great.

VII. THE GOAT SUCKER.

An evil name should never be given except it is deserved.

"When you can only see," says Waterton, "a straggler or two of the feathered tribe hastening to join its mate already at its roosting place, the goat sucker comes out of the forest, where it has sat all day long in slumbering ease, unmindful of the gay and busy scenes around it. Its eyes are too delicately formed to bear the light; and thus it is forced to shun the flaming face of day, and wait in patience till night invites him to partake of her pleasures.

" The harmless, unoffending goat sucker, from the time of Aristotle down to the present day, has been in disgrace with man. Father has handed down to son, and author to author, that this bird subsists by milking flocks. But how sadly has it suffered !

" When the moon shines bright, you may see it close by the cows, goats, and sheep, jumping up every now and then under their bellies. Approach a little nearer, he is not shy ;

'He fears no danger, for he knows no sin.'

See how the nocturnal flies are tormenting the herd, and with what dexterity he springs up and catches them as fast as they alight on the belly, legs, and udder of the animals. Observe how quiet they stand, and how sensible they seem of his good offices; for they neither strike at him, nor hit him with their tail, nor tread on him, nor try to drive him away as an uncivil intruder. Were you to dissect him, and inspect his stomach, you would find no milk there. It is full of the flies which have been annoying the herd."

APPLICATION.

Animals have often suffered from an evil name. You think, perhaps, you may kick that dog, because he growled and bit one of your play fellows the other day, and thus was called mischievous or spiteful; but have you forgotten that he did this only when he was teased, and struck, and ill treated? Beside, how often has he shown his pleasure at your approach, and how faithfully has he watched your dwelling!

Or it may be, you think, you may wantonly beat that poor ass, because you have heard it called stupid and wayward; yet how patiently has it carried you, and how freely has it yielded its nourishing milk! Had it always been treated kindly, it might now have been very tractable. An old man, who a few years ago sold vegetables in London, used an ass, which conveyed his baskets from door to door. Frequently he gave the poor creature a handful of hay, or some pieces of bread or greens, by way of refreshment and reward. The old man had no need of any goad for the animal, and seldom indeed had he to lift up his hand to drive it on. This kind treatment was one day remarked to him, and he was asked whether his beast was apt to be stubborn. " Ah, master," he replied, "it is of no use to be cruel; and as for stubbornness I cannot complain, for he is ready to do any thing, or go any where. He is sometimes skittish and playful, and once ran away from me : you will hardly believe it, but there were more than fifty people after him, attempting in vain to stop him ; yet he turned back of himself, and never stopped till he ran his head kindly into my bosom."

An evil name should never be applied until it is deserved. A child has sometimes been called cross or ill tempered, and has, in consequence, been shunned by others, when, but for this injustice and disregard of truth, it would have been found far otherwise. Never reproach another for doing wrong unless you are *quite sure* he has done it—every one should be treated as innocent until he is proved to be guilty, and even then he should not be made out worse than he is.

VIII. THE NEW ZEALANDERS.
People are to be esteemed not according to the Dress, but the Mind.

THE New Zealanders are fond of dress: to a chief, who came on board the Active, Mr. Marsden presented a piece of India print, which quite transported him with delight; he gazed on the figures with the greatest amazement, and throwing it over his shoulders, strutted about the deck with his whole soul absorbed in his splendid garb. On another occasion, Mr. Nicholas being on shore, and engaged in making purchases, was assailed by an old man, who offered him a large mat for his coat; to this he agreed. No sooner had the islander adjusted the coat on his own person, than his whole being seemed to have undergone a change. Mr. Marsden, too, in the journal of his second visit, mentions that he was much importuned by his friend Moodeenty, one of the chiefs, for a red flannel shirt, a night cap, and a pair of spectacles. He observed that, if he could only get these articles, he should be a great man. And the ferocious Shungie mentioned, as one of his grievances on his return from England, that he had not a piece of scarlet cloth, such as other chiefs possessed. " I gave him a piece to-day," adds the relator, " which seemed for the time, to set his mind at rest; he put it over his shoulders, and strutted about with the consequence of a Roman emperor."

APPLICATION.

You smile contemptuously, perhaps, at savages, and think their love of dress very ridiculous. You see that their clothes can make no real alteration in them ; that however fine they appear, their language and manners must always betray their uncivilized state.

And yet it may be *you* are fond of finery. Many think if they have clothes of the same colour or shape as their superiors, they will be taken for *them;* but their attempts to deceive are sure to be detected. Persons of true rank and dignity often care little about dress; and, certainly, many things are far more desirable than fine clothes. When the celebrated Erasmus was a poor student at Paris, he was indeed very anxious to be a little richer; but almost in rags as he was, it was not fine, nor even comfortable raiment, after which he principally longed. " As soon as I get money," says he, in a letter to a friend, " I will buy, first, Greek books, and then clothes." He felt, it is said, that " it is the mind that makes the body rich."

IX. THE MORA.

Avoid the beginning of Evil.

THE wild fig tree, which is as large as a common English apple tree, often rears itself from one of the thick branches at the top of the mora ; and when its fruit is ripe, the birds resort to it for nourishment. To a seed deposited by a bird, which had perched on the mora, the fig tree first owed its elevated station ; but now, in its turn, it is doomed to contribute a portion of its own sap and juices toward the growth of different species of vines, the seeds of which, also, the birds deposited on the branches. These soon vegetate and bear fruit in great quantities; so that, with their taking the resources of the fig tree, and the fig tree those of the mora; the mora, unable to support the burden, languishes and dies; and then the fig tree and its usurping vines, receiving no more succour from their late foster parent, droop and perish in their turn.

APPLICATION.

One evil makes way for another. A falsehood, for example, often needs another for its concealment; and he who utters it, discovers so little regard for what is right, as to excite fear that he will not refuse, should temptation arise, to do any thing else that is wrong. So too, a covetous disposition has led to a petty theft, and this to others, until the awful crime of murder has been committed, and the transgressor has been plunged into ruin. Thus,—

"The first crime pass'd compels us into more,
And guilt grows fate that was but choice before."

"With many persons," says D'Argonne, "the early age of life is passed in sowing in their minds the vices that are most suitable to their inclinations; and the middle age goes on in nourishing and maturing these vices; and the last age concludes in gathering in pain and anguish, the bitter fruit of these wretched seeds." He, then, that would not continue to do evil, must guard against doing it once; and he who would avoid an evil act, must strive against an evil feeling and an evil thought.

X. DR. MURRAY AND MR. GIFFORD.

Important Ends may be accomplished by humble Means ; but when it is practicable the best should be employed.

THE celebrated Dr. Alexander Murray received from his father, who was a shepherd, his first lessons in reading, in his sixth year. The old man bought him a catechism ; (which, in Scotland, is generally printed with a copy of the alphabet in a large type ;) "but as it was too good a book," says he, "for me to handle at all times, it was generally locked up ; and he, throughout the winter, drew the figures of the letters to me, in his *written* hand, on the board of an old *wool card,* with the black end of an extinguished heather stem or root, snatched from the fire. I soon learned all the alphabet in this form, and became a *writer* as well as *reader.* I wrought with the *board* and *brand* continually."

Mr. Gifford, who rose to great eminence, says: "I possessed but one book in the world; it was a treatise on algebra, given to me by a young woman, who found it in a lodging house. I considered it as a treasure ; but it was a treasure locked up, for it supposed the reader to be well acquainted with what I knew nothing of.

"My master's son had purchased Jennings's Introduction ; this was precisely what I wanted, but he carefully concealed it from

me, and I was indebted to chance alone for
stumbling upon his hiding place. I sat up for
the greatest part of several nights succes-
sively, and before he suspected that his treatise was discovered, had completely mastered
it. I could now enter upon my own, and that
carried me pretty far into the science. This
was not done without difficulty. I had not a
farthing on earth, nor a friend to give me one ;
pen, ink, and paper, therefore, were, for the
most part, as completely out of my reach as
a crown and sceptre. There was indeed a
resource ; but the utmost caution and secrecy
were necessary in applying to it. I beat out
pieces of leather as smooth as possible, and
wrought my problems on them with a blunted
awl ; for the rest my memory was tenacious,
and I could multiply and divide by it to a
great extent."

APPLICATION.

These are striking proofs that "necessity
is the mother of invention," and that "where
there's a will there's a way." The success of
these eminent persons should urge others not
to despond in unfavourable circumstances,
but to strain every nerve to accomplish an
important object. And then how do they
shame many who care nothing about knowledge, or are sluggish in its pursuit ! Still it
is no merit to accomplish an object by difficult instruments when easy ones are at hand,
or to reach an end by a circuitous course,

when there is a straight road. Michael Angelo, being told of an artist who painted with his fingers, exclaimed, "Why does not the blockhead use his pencils?" And a modern traveller remarks, as he passed along the banks of the Oult, or Oulta, "That they should use wood in the southern parts, where there is no stone to be found, is not surprising; but here, where all is rock, it seems strange perverseness not to use it. It would only be to remove the stones from one side, where they are still an obstruction, to the other, where the stones have fallen away, and a permanent road is made; but, instead of this, they make flat forms of boards, which are continually decaying, so that the greater part of the road for six miles, is a tottering wooden scaffolding over a precipice."

XI. THE ISLAND WARRIORS.

Many are seriously injured by fright.

MR. ELLIS, who spent some days at the Bay of Islands, noticed among the New Zealanders a disposition to terrify by way of joke. "The warriors," says he, "delight in swaggering and bravado, and while my companion was talking with some of Korro-Korro's party, one of them came up to me, and several times brandished his patoo-patoo over my head, as if intending to strike, accompanying the action with the fiercest expressions of countenance, and the utterance of words exceedingly harsh, though to me unintelligible. After a few minutes he desisted, but when we walked away, he ran after us, and, assuming the same attitude and gestures, accompanied us till we reached another circle, where he continued for a short time these exhibitions of his skill in terrifying. When he ceased, he inquired rather significantly if I was not afraid. I told him I was unconscious of having offended him, and that, notwithstanding his actions, I did not think he intended to injure me. The New Zealanders are fond of endeavouring to alarm strangers, and appear to derive much satisfaction in witnessing the indications of fear they are able to excite."

APPLICATION.

Many children are in this respect like the New Zealanders. They get behind doors, and dart out suddenly and unexpectedly on others—wear frightful clothes and masks—look as if they were very angry, and threaten to beat violently the young and the timid. Now all this is wrong. Some have been terrified into fits—others have lost their reason—and not a few have died in consequence of these foolish and wicked tricks. Surely, then, if you have ever played them, you will think of this, and never do so again.

XII. PETER THE GREAT, OBERLIN, AND RUPP.

Things declared to be impossible may be done.

"*It is impossible!*" said some, when Peter the Great determined on a voyage of discovery, and the cold and uninhabited region over which he reigned furnished nothing but some larch trees to construct his vessels. But though the iron, the cordage, the sails, and all that was necessary, except the provisions for victual- ling them, were to be carried through the im- mense deserts of Siberia—down rivers of dif- ficult navigation—and along roads almost impassable—*the thing was done ;* for the com- mand of the sovereign and the perseverance of the people surmounted every obstacle.

"*It is impossible!*" said some, as soon as they heard of a scheme of Oberlin's.—To res- cue his parishioners from a half-savage state, he determined to open a communication with the high road to Strasbourg, so that the pro- ductions of the Ban de la Roche might find a market. Having assembled the people, he proposed that they should blast the rocks, and convey a sufficient quantity of enormous mas- ses to construct a wall for a road about a mile and a half in length along the Banks of the river Bruche, and build a bridge across it near Rothan. The peasants were astonished at his proposition, and pronounced it imprac- ticable, and every one excused himself on the ground of private business. He, however, reasoned with them, and added the offer of his own example. No sooner had he pronounced these words, than, with a pickaxe on his shoulder, he proceeded to the spot, while the astonished peasants, animated by his example, forgot their excuses, and hastened with one consent to fetch their tools to follow him. At length every obstacle was surmounted— walls were erected to support the earth, which appeared ready to give way—mountain torrents, which had hitherto inundated the meadows, were diverted into courses, or received into beds sufficient to contain them ; and *the thing was done.* The bridge still bears the name of " *Le Pont de Charité*"—the Bridge of Charity.

" *It is impossible !*" said some, as they looked at the impenetrable forests which covered the rugged flanks and deep gorges of Mount Pilatus, in Switzerland, and hearkened to the daring plan of a man named Rupp—to convey the pines from the top of the mountain to the lake of Lucerne, a distance of nearly nine miles. Without being discouraged by their exclamations, he formed a slide, or trough, of twenty-four thousand pine trees, six feet broad, and from three to six feet deep ; and this slide, which was completed in 1812, (and called the slide of Alpnach, from the name of the place where it was situated,) was kept moist. Its length was forty-four thousand English feet. It had to be conducted over rocks, or along their sides, or under ground, or over deep gorges where it was sustained by scaffoldings, and yet skill and perseverance overcame every obstacle,—*and the thing was done.* The trees rolled down from the mountain into the lake with wonderful rapidity. The larger pines, which were about a hundred feet long, ran through the space of eight miles and a third in about six minutes. A gentleman, who saw this great work, says, that " such was the speed with which a tree of the largest size passed any given point, that he could only strike it once with a stick as it rushed by, however quickly he attempted to repeat the blow."

APPLICATION.

Say not hastily then—" it is impossible!" It may be so to do a thing in an hour, a day, or a week ; or by thoughtlessness, carelessness, and indolence ; but to act with wisdom, energy, and perseverance, is to insure success. " Time and patience," says a Spanish author, " make the mulberry leaf satin !" And Periander remarks, that " care and industry do every thing."

XIII. THE FIRE FLY.

Avoid all unkindness and cruelty.

As Waterton urges some one to visit the wilds of Demarara, he says,—" If thou hast but courage to set about giving the world a finished picture of it, neither materials to work on, nor colours to paint it in its true shades will be wanting to thee. It may appear a difficult task at a distance; but look close at it, and it is nothing at all; provided thou hast but a quiet mind, little more is necessary. Thou mayest slay the fawn, and cut down the mountain cabbage for thy support, and select from every part of the domain whatever may be necessary for the work thou art about; but having killed a pair of doves in order to enable thee to give mankind a true and proper description of them, thou must not destroy a third through wantonness, or to show what a good marksman thou art; that would only blot the picture thou art finishing, not colour it.

" At noon, thou mayest go to the troely, one leaf of which will defend thee from both sun and rain. And if, in the cool of the evening, thou hast been tempted to stray too far from thy place of abode, and art deprived of light to write down the information thou hast collected, the fire fly, which thou wilt see in almost every bush around thee will be thy candle. Hold it over thy pocket book, in any position which thou knowest will not hurt it, and it will afford thee ample light. And when thou hast done with it, put it kindly back again on the next branch to thee. It will want no other reward for its services."

APPLICATION.

I should like to read this to all those children who are unkind and cruel. And such are those who pull off the legs or wings of flies—run pins through cockchafers —plunder birds' nests—teaze the dogs and cats about them—or plague and torment the asses or ponies they ride. Ah! they would cry, and call me very cruel and wicked, were I to come and pull their hair, or draw their teeth, or whip them with a rod; and what would they say were I to take up that little babe from the cradle, and pinch its cheeks or its arms, when it cannot get away from me, or tell what I have done? Go then, my little boy, and be cruel no more; but remember that those should be treated with special tenderness, who are helpless, and cannot defend themselves, and do not and cannot complain.

XIV. THE MISSIONARIES' SERVANT.

Sound is often mistaken for sense.

FATHER LAFITAU and his brother missionaries, while residing among the Hurons of North America, had a servant who did not know a word of the language of the Indians, but had caught what may be called its accent, very correctly, so that he could give a good imitation of its general effect on the ear; and this man, merely to amuse himself, was wont to make long speeches to the savages, in a jargon literally having no meaning whatever, but only pronounced in their own tone, which they used to hear with great attention, and never doubted were addresses in their own language, only his style of oratory, they said, was so elevated that they could not always comprehend him.

APPLICATION.

Others, beside these people, often mistake sound for sense. Many words and phrases in common use mean nothing. How often do people say—" I am *extremely* glad," without feeling any pleasure—" I am *exceedingly* sorry," without feeling any grief—or "I am *greatly* obliged," without feeling that any favour has been conferred! If then you suppose you may believe all they utter, you will be frequently deceived. But whatever others do, remember it becomes you at all times to say what you mean, and to mean what you say : for this is required by common propriety; and it is written, that "for every idle word we speak, we must give account in the day of judgment."

———

XV. THE BEAVERS.

Union is strength.

BEAVERS generally choose a pond, or a piece of ground with a stream running through it; but to form a dam, it is necessary that they should stop the stream, and of course that they should know in what direction it runs. They always, however, choose the most favourable place, and never begin at a wrong part. They drive stakes five or six feet long into the ground, in different rows, and interweave them with branches of trees, filling them up with clay, stones, and sand. The dams are sometimes a hundred feet long, ten or twelve feet thick at the base, exactly level from end to end, perpendicular toward the stream, and sloped on the outside, where grass soon grows, and renders the earth more united.

At the head of one of the rivers of Louisiana, M. du Pratz found a beaver dam in a very retired place, and ordered one of his men to cut, as silently as possible, a gutter about a foot wide through it, and to retire immediately. "As soon as the water through the gutter began to make a noise, (says the writer,) we heard a beaver come from one of the huts and plunge in. We saw him get on the bank, and clearly perceived that he examined it. He then, with all his force, gave four distinct blows with his tail, when immediately the whole colony threw themselves into the water, and arrived upon the dam. As soon as they were assembled, one of them appeared, by muttering, to issue some kind of order, for they all instantly left the place, and went out on the banks of the pond in different directions. Those nearest to us were between our station and the den, and therefore we could observe their operations very plainly. Some of them formed a substance resembling a kind of mortar; others carried this on their tails, which served as sledges for the purpose. I observed that they put themselves two and two, and that each of a couple loaded his fellow. They trailed the mortar, which was pretty stiff, quite to the dam, where others were stationed to take it; these put it into the gutter, and rammed it down with blows of their tails. The noise of the water soon ceased, and the breach was completely repaired. One of the beavers then struck two blows with his tail, and instantly they all took to the water without any noise, and disappeared."

APPLICATION.

That will be well done in a family or community in which every one does his part. The humble may do unitedly what the highest cannot do singly. Skill is valuable, but success is often the reward of order and harmony as well as of energy and perseverance.

XVI. THE TURKEY COCK.

Mind your own business.

A FEMALE turkey belonging to a gentleman in Sweden was once sitting upon eggs; and as the cock in her absence began to appear uneasy and dejected, he was put into the place with her. He immediately sat down by her side, and it was soon found that he had taken some eggs from under her, and had himself sat on them. The eggs were put back; but he soon afterward took them again. This induced the owner, by way of experiment, to have a nest made, and as many eggs put into it as it was thought the cock could conveniently cover. The bird seemed highly pleased with this mark of confidence; he sat with great patience on the eggs, and was so attentive to the hatching them, as scarcely to afford himself time to take the food necessary for his support. At the usual period, twenty-eight young ones were produced; but the cock was not a little perplexed and troubled on seeing so many little creatures picking around him, and requiring his care. So the brood was reared by other means.

APPLICATION.

It is not well for us always to have our own way. Were our wishes gratified, we should often find, even after they had cost us much pains, that they only yielded trouble. He will be most happy whose great concern is to do what is required of him; he will be most wretched who neglects this to meddle with other things.

XVII. THE WASPS.

Kindness may sometimes appear to be cruelty.

ABOUT the beginning of October, the wasps not only cease to bring nourishment to their young, but drag the grubs from their cells, and carry them out of the nest, where, exposed to the weather, and deprived of food, they all unavoidably perish, should the wasps neglect, as they seldom do, to kill them with their fangs. And perhaps you say, " How cruel this is!" But no! it is probably the greatest compassion that could have been shown. Wasps are not, like honey bees, endowed with the instinct of laying up a store of provisions for the winter. Were they not therefore at once destroyed by their parents, the young ones must necessarily die a cruel and lingering death, occasioned by hunger!

APPLICATION.

Some things may appear at first sight strange and cruel, but they do not when the reason of them is known. It may *seem* cruel to kill a dog,—but it is not if he is mad. It may *seem* cruel to give a child nauseous medicine,—but it is not if he is ill, and this is necessary to health. It may *seem* cruel to punish a little boy by making him learn an extra task, or keeping him in school, or giving him some stripes on the hand or the back,—but it is not if he will not learn without, and but for this would be a dunce. Many persons are very kind who give pain : those only are cruel who do so for the sake of making others suffer; and it would be well for them to remember, that " no one ever did a designed injury to another, without doing a greater to himself."

XVIII. THE CHAMOIS HUNTER.

Danger should only be encountered when it is unavoidable, and to face it is praiseworthy.

THE chamois hunter knows no danger: he crosses the snows, without thinking of the abysses they may cover ; he plunges into the most dangerous passes of the mountains—he climbs up, he leaps from rock to rock, without considering how he can return. The night often finds him in the heat of the pursuit; but he does not give it up for this obstacle. He considers that the chamois will stop during the darkness, as well as himself, and that on the morrow he may again reach them. He passes the night, not at the foot of a tree, nor in a cave covered with verdure, as does the hunter of the plain,—but upon a naked rock, or upon a heap of rough stones, without any sort of shelter. He is alone, without fire,

without light; but he takes from his bag a bit
of cheese and some of the barley bread, which
is his ordinary food—bread so hard that he is
obliged to break it between two stones, or to
cleave it with the axe which he always carries with him to cut steps, which shall serve
for his ladder up rocks of ice. His frugal
meal soon ended, he puts a stone under his
head, and is presently asleep, dreaming of the
way the chamois has taken. He is awakened
by the freshness of the morning air; he rises,
pierced through with cold; he measures with
his eyes the precipices which he must yet
climb to reach the chamois; he drinks a little
brandy, (of which he always carries a small
provision,) throws his bag across his shoulder,
and again rushes forward to encounter new
dangers. These daring and persevering hunters often remain whole days in the dreariest
solitudes of the glaciers of Chamouni; and
during this time their families, and, above all,
their unhappy wives, feel the keenest alarm
for their safety. And yet, with the full knowledge of the dangers to be encountered, the
chase of the chamois is the object of a strong
passion.

Saussure knew a handsome young man of
the district of Chamouni, who was about to be
married; and the adventurous hunter thus ad-
dressed the naturalist:—"My grandfather was
killed in the chase of the chamois; my father
was killed also; and I am so certain that I shall
be killed, that I call this bag, which I always

carry in hunting, my winding sheet: I am
sure that I shall have no other; and yet, if
you were to offer to make my fortune, upon
the condition that I should renounce the chase
of the chamois, I should refuse your kindness."
Saussure adds, that he went several journeys
in the Alps with this young man; that he possessed astonishing skill and strength; but that
his temerity was greater than either; and that
two years after he met the fate he anticipated,
by his foot failing on the brink of a precipice
to which he had leaped.

APPLICATION.

Danger must sometimes be encountered.
The life of the soldier, the sailor, the traveller,
necessarily exposes to peril; and there are
times, when, in the defence of themselves or
their property, or to shield the persons and
possessions of others, people ought to face it.
But wisdom teaches that the object aimed at
should always be worth the effort. It is not
so with the chamois hunter; he likes the dangers of the chase, and cares but little about
the prey. And so children are often as un-
wise, or even more so: one will try to walk
on the edge of a plank, or a wall—another
will light a piece of paper to watch how long
it will burn before it reaches his fingers—and
what use is this? Beside, the one may fall
to the ground, and the clothes of the other
may take fire; and then they will deserve
to be punished for their folly, rather than to

be pitied for their pain. " If," says Quarles, " thou desire to be truly valiant, fear to do any injury : he that fears not to do evil, is always afraid to suffer evil: he that never fears is desperate, and he that always fears is a coward. He is truly valiant who dares nothing but what he may, and fears nothing but what he ought."

XIX. THE ESQUIMAUX.

Unfavourable circumstances have some alleviations.

THE inhabitants of the shores of Baffin's Bay, and of those still more inclement regions to which our discovery ships have recently penetrated, are, perhaps, not destined to advance much farther than their present condition in the scale of humanity. Their climate forbids their attempting the gratification of any desires beyond the commonest animal wants. In the short summers they hunt reindeer for a stock of food and clothing ; during the long winter, when the stern demands of hunger drive them from their snow huts to search for provisions, they still find a supply in the reindeer, in the seals which lie in holes under the ice of the lakes, and in the bears which prowl about on the frozen shores of the sea. But without the fine scent and undaunted courage of their dogs, the several objects of their chase would never be obtained in sufficient quantities, during the winter, to supply the wants of the inhabitants; nor could the men be conveyed from place to place, over the snow, with that celerity which greatly contributes to their success in hunting. In drawing the sledges, if the dogs scent a single reindeer, even a quarter of a mile distant, they gallop off furiously in the direction of the scent, and the animal is soon within reach of the unerring arrow of the hunter. They will discover a seal hole, entirely by the smell, at a very great distance. Their desire to attack the ferocious bear is so great, that the word *ninnock*, which signifies that animal, is often used to encourage them when running in a sledge: two or three dogs, led forward by a man, will fasten upon the largest bear without hesitation. They are eager to chase every animal but the wolf; and of him they appear to have an instinctive terror, which manifests itself on his approach in a loud and continued howl. Probably there is no animal which combines so many properties useful to his master, as the dog of the Esquimaux.

APPLICATION.

We may sometimes think our case hard; but it might soon be far worse. The Esquimaux appear necessitous; but how much more needy would they be without their dogs! Let us, then, make the best of what we have, and refrain from coveting what is denied us. No station can be allotted us in providence in which the reasons are not many for contentment and gratitude. Every trial we have to bear has some alleviation.

XX. THE BEAR.

Parental affection is strong and tender.

While the *Carcase* frigate, which went out some years ago to make discoveries toward the north pole, was locked in the ice, the man at the masthead gave notice, early one morning, that three bears were directing their course toward the ship. They had no doubt been invited by the scent of the blubber of a sea horse that the crew had killed a few days before, which had been set on fire, and was burning on the ice at the time of their approach. They proved to be a she bear and her two cubs; but the cubs were nearly as large as the dam. They ran eagerly to the fire, and drew out of the flames part of the flesh of the sea horse that remained unconsumed, and ate it voraciously. The crew threw great lumps of the flesh of the sea horse, which they had still remaining, on the ice. These the old bear fetched away singly, laid every lump before her cubs as she brought it, and dividing it. gave to each a share, reserving for herself but a small portion. As she was fetching away the last piece, the sailors levelled their muskets at the cubs, and shot them both dead; and in her retreat they wounded the dam, but not mortally. It would have drawn tears of pity from any but the most unfeeling, to have marked the affectionate concern expressed by this poor beast in the last moments of her expiring young. Though she was herself dreadfully wounded, and could but just crawl to the place where they lay, she carried the lump of flesh she had fetched away, as she had done others before, tore it in pieces, and laid it before them ; and, when she saw that they refused to eat, she laid her paws first upon one, and then upon the other, and endeavoured to raise them up, all the while moaning most piteously. When she found she could not stir them, she went off; and, when she had got to some distance, looked back and moaned; and that not availing her to entice them away, she returned, and smelling round them, began to lick their wounds. She went off a second time as before; and having crawled a few paces, looked again behind her, and for some time stood moaning. But still her cubs not rising to follow her, she returned to them again, and with signs of inexpressible fondness, went round pawing them and moaning. Finding at last that they were cold and lifeless, she raised her head toward the ship and uttered a growl of despair, which the crew returned in a volley of musket balls. She fell between her cubs, and died licking their wounds !

APPLICATION.

The absence of parental affection degrades a man or woman below the brutes. This,

however, is happily but seldom discovered.
The love of parents to their children is commonly strong and ardent, or children, the
most needy and helpless of creatures, would
perish in multitudes. How obedient and
affectionate then ought children to be to
those who love them so tenderly and constantly!

XXI. THE HAWTHORN.

Strange tales are not always true.

COMMON hawthorn, or white thorn, is valuable both as a hedge shrub and as a tree. Few
plants exceed it in beauty when in bloom ; the
season of which is usually May ; on which
account the name of May, or "May blossom,"
is in some places given to the tree. There is
one variety, however, the Glastonbury thorn,
(to which the monks of the dark ages attached
a popular legend,) that flowers in January
or February, and in favourable seasons and
situations, as early as Christmas. Gilpin
mentions, that one of its progeny, which grew
in the gardens at Bulstrode, had its flower
buds perfectly formed so early as the 21st of
December. In the royal gardens at Kew,
a similar thorn flowers at the same season.
The belief that certain trees put forth their
flowers on Christmas day, was not confined
to the Glastonbury thorn. In the New Forest, at Cadenham, near Lyndhurst, an oak
used to bud about that period ; but the people

for many years believed that it never budded
all the year, except on old Christmas day.
The superstition was destroyed by careful in-
vestigation ; and the circumstance is thus recorded in the Salisbury newspaper, of Jan. 10,
1786 :—" In consequence of a report that has
prevailed in this county for upward of two
centuries, and which, by many, has been considered as a matter of faith, that the oak at
Cadenham, in the New Forest, shoots forth
leaves on every old Christmas day, and that
no leaf is ever to be seen on it either before
or after that day during the winter, a lady,
who is now on a visit in this city, and who is
attentively curious to every thing relative to
art or nature, made a journey to Cadenham,
on Monday, the 3d instant, purposely to inquire on the spot about the production of this
famous tree. On her arrival near it, the
usual guide was ready to attend her ; but on
his being desired to climb the oak, and to
search whether there were any leaves then
on it, he said it would be to no purpose ; but
that if she would come on the Wednesday following (Christmas day,) she might certainly
see thousands. However, he was prevailed
upon to ascend, and on the first branch which
he gathered, appeared several fair new leaves,
fresh sprouted from the buds, and nearly an
inch and a half in length. It may be imagin-
ed that the guide was more amazed at this
premature production than the lady ; for, so
strong was his belief in the truth of the whole

tradition, that he would have pledged his life
that not a leaf was to have been discovered
on any part of the tree before the usual hour."

APPLICATION.

Never listen to tales merely because they
are very strange and wonderful. Some true
things are strange, but many strange things
are not true. The hyena, for instance, possesses great strength in the neck; and
for this reason, Pliny and other ancient wri-
ters believed that his neck consisted of one
bone without any joint. Shaw tells us that
the Arabs, when they kill a hyena, bury the
head, lest it should be made the means of
some charm against their safety and happiness. The Greeks and Romans believed too,
that the hyena imitated the human voice, (the
popular name of *laughing* hyena is perhaps
derived from this notion,) and that it had the
power of charming the shepherds, so as to
rivet them to the spot on which they were met
by the quadruped, in the same way that a
serpent fascinates a bird. It has also been
gravely maintained, that the elephant had no
joints, and, being unable to lie down, slept
standing against a tree;—that the badger had
the legs of one side shorter than those of the
other;—that deer lived several hundred
years;—that the chameleon derived its support solely from atmospheric air;—that birds
of paradise never touched the ground, lived
wholly on dew, were produced without legs,

and hung themselves by the two long feathers of the tail to the branch of a tree;—that the salamander owed its existence to the purest of elements, so that it was called "the daughter of fire;" though it was said to have a body of ice, and that were one of these small lizards thrown into the flame, in the most raging conflagration, its progress would be immediately checked. Thus many strange tales are to be traced to falsehood, credulity, or folly. Regard then what is told you by a man of wisdom and truth, but "go from the presence of a foolish man, when thou perceivest not in him the words of knowledge."

XXII. THE ICHNEUMON.

Evil dispositions may break out, though for a time concealed.

"I had," says M. D'Obsonville, "an ichneumon very young, which I brought up; I fed it at first with milk, and afterward with baked meat mixed with rice. It soon became even tamer than a cat; for it came when called, and followed me, though at liberty, into the country.

"One day I brought him a small water serpent alive, being desirous to know how far his instinct would carry him against a creature with which he was hitherto totally unacquainted. His first emotion seemed to be astonishment, mixed with anger, for his hairs became erect; but in an instant after he step-

ped behind the reptile, and with a remarkable
swiftness and agility leaped upon its head,
seized it, and crushed it between his teeth.
This effort and new food seemed to have
awakened his inward and destructive vora-
city, which, till then, had given way to the
gentleness he had acquired from his education.

"I had about my house several curious
kinds of fowls, among which he had been
brought up, and which, till then, he had suffered to go and come unmolested and unre-
garded; but a few days after, when he found
himself alone, he strangled them every one,
ate a little, and, as appeared, drank the blood
of two."

APPLICATION.

It is one thing to restrain evil dispositions;
it is another to have them rooted out. Many
things may keep children from the grossest
wickedness, but unless *He* who made the
heart changes it, its depravity will break
forth; and there is nothing, however bad,
which they may not do at some time or other.
What we really are is not to be learned from
what we *appear* when the eyes of others are
upon us, but from what we *are* when following our own will.

XXIII. THE DESERT.

Common things are often undervalued.

BELZONI, the celebrated traveller, states, that in a desert, generally speaking, there are few springs of water, some of them at the distance of four, six, and eight days' journey from one another, and not all of sweet water; on the contrary, it is generally salt or bitter; so that if the thirsty traveller drinks of it, it increases his thirst, and he suffers more than before. But when the calamity happens, that the next well, which is so anxiously sought for, is found dry, the misery of such a situation cannot be well described. The camels, which afford the only means of escape, are so thirsty that they cannot proceed to another well; and if the travellers kill them, to extract the little liquid which remains in their stomachs, they themselves cannot advance any farther. The situation must be dreadful, and admits of no resource. Many perish, victims of most horrible thirst. It is then that the value of a cup of water is really felt. In such a case there is no distinction. If the master has none, the servant will not give it to him ; for very few are the instances where a man will voluntarily lose his life to save that of another, particularly in a caravan in the desert, where people are strangers to each other. What a situation for a man, though a rich one, perhaps the owner of all the caravans ! He is dying for a cup of water—no one gives it to him ; he offers all he possesses—no one hears him ; they are all dying—though by walking a few hours farther, they might be saved. If the camels are lying down and cannot be made to rise—no one has strength to walk—only he that has a glass of that precious liquor lives to walk a mile farther, and perhaps dies too. If the voyages on seas are dangerous, so are those in the deserts. At sea, the provisions very often fail—in the desert it is worse ; at sea, storms are met with—in the desert there cannot be a greater storm than to find a dry well ; at sea one meets with pirates—we escape—we surrender—we die ; in the desert they rob the traveller of all his property and water ; they let him live perhaps—but what a life ! to die the most barbarous and agonizing death ! In short, to be thirsty in a desert, without water —exposed to the burning sun, without shelter—and with no hopes of finding either, is the most terrible situation that a man can be placed in, and one of the greatest sufferings that a human being can sustain ;—the eyes grow inflamed ; the tongue and lips swell ; a hollow sound is heard in the ears, which brings on deafness ; and the brains appear to grow thick and inflamed :—all these feelings arise from *the want of a little water.*

APPLICATION.

How little are our common mercies valued! Their frequent enjoyment ought to increase our gratitude ; but instead of this, it is perverted to produce insensibility to their worth. Let us learn, however, that if a little water may be so precious, how great are *our* obligations to the Giver of all, who have not only what is necessary to the support of life, but to its comfort also.

XXIV. THE SLOTH.

Praise is often due where censure is given.

THE sloth, when placed on the ground, seems strangely and awkwardly formed. His fore legs, or, more correctly speaking, his arms, are apparently much too long, while his hind legs are very short, and look as if they could be bent almost to the shape of a corkscrew ; so that when put on the floor, his belly touches the ground. Suppose, then, he

supported himself on his legs, like other animals, he would be in pain, for he has no soles
to his feet, and his claws are very sharp, and
long, and curved, so that were his body supported by his feet, it would be by their extremi-
ties,—just as your body would be, were you to
throw yourself on all fours, and try to support
it on the ends of your toes and fingers! Were
the floor of glass, or of a polished surface, the
sloth would actually be quite stationary; but
as the ground is generally rough, with little
risings upon it, from stones, roots of grass,
&c., this just suits him, and he moves his fore
legs in all directions, in order to find something to lay hold of; and when he has suc-
ceeded, he pulls himself forward, and is thus
enabled to travel onward, but at the same
time in so tardy and awkward a manner, as
to acquire him the name of sloth. Indeed, his
looks and gestures show his uncomfortable
situation; and as a sigh every now and then
escapes him, we may be entitled to conclude
that he is actually in pain.

But mark! The sloth, in its wild state,
spends its whole life in trees, and never leaves
them but through force or by accident. An
all-ruling Providence has ordered man to tread
on the surface of the earth, the eagle to soar
in the expanse of the skies, and the monkey
and squirrel to inhabit the trees; still these
may change their relative situations without
feeling much inconvenience; but the sloth is
doomed to spend his whole life in the trees;

and, what is more extraordinary, *not upon the branches*, like the squirrel and the monkey, nor does he hang head downward, like the vampire, but *under the branches*. When asleep, he supports himself from a branch parallel to the earth. He first seizes the branch with one arm, and then with the other; and after that brings up both his legs, one by one, to the same branch, so that all four are in a line; and in this position he seems perfectly at rest. Now, had he a tail, he would be at a loss to know what to do with it: were he to draw it up within his legs, it would interfere with them; and were he to let it hang down, it would become the sport of the winds. His tail scarcely exceeds an inch and a half in length, and its shortness is a benefit to him.

One day, Waterton, whose description we have given, found a large two-toed sloth on the ground, upon the bank of the Essequibo. "As soon as we got up to him," he says, "he threw himself upon his back, and defended himself in gallant style with his fore legs. 'Come, poor fellow,' said I to him, 'if thou hast got into a hobble to-day, thou shalt not suffer for it. I'll take no advantage of thee in misfortune; the forest is large enough both for me and thee to rove in; go thy ways up above, and enjoy thyself in these endless wilds; it is more than probable thou wilt never have another interview with man; so fare thee well.' On saying this, I took a long stick which was lying there, held it for him to hook on, and then

conveyed him to a high and stately mora. He
ascended with wonderful rapidity, and in about
a minute he was almost at the top of the tree.
He now went off in a side direction, and caught
hold of the branch of a neighbouring tree; he
then proceeded toward the heart of the forest.

" Thus I felt persuaded that the world has
hitherto erred in its conjectures concerning the
sloth, from descriptions being given of him *on
the ground*, and not in the only position in
which he ought to have been described, name-
ly, *clinging to the branch of a tree.*"

APPLICATION.

" What an odd-looking fellow that is," says
a town boy, as he sees one who has just come
from a distant village; " and then how awkward he is; how sheepish he looks; how he
strokes down his hair; and how he throws
out his legs when he walks !"

Let me say for him, then, you see him *out of his place.* Were you to go back with him, you would find he could plough, and reap, and thrash, and look after the sheep and cattle, and support his aged mother by his earnings; and *this is more than you could do!*

" What do you think," says the country boy, " of that cockneỳ lad? Why he knows nothing! Father put him on our Jack, and how he looked! why I could ride better when I was three years old! Ha! ha! ha! And then he thought them clipped hedges grew so! and that we cut wheat with a scythe—and—and—"

Stop, my boy, you have not yet seen him *at home,* and in a farmer's house *he is out of his place.* He reads nicely, he writes beautifully, he cyphers well, and he can tell you all about the kings of England; and mention all the mountains and rivers, and productions of the earth—and *this is what you could not do.*

Children and people, then, are to be judged of when they are in that state for which nature or instruction has designed them. A weaver would make a poor blacksmith; a carpenter would make a poor tailor; and yet each of them, kept to his place, may do his work well: and no one is to be blamed for the want of what he never had an opportunity of acquiring.

XXV. THE LION.

*Gratitude is delightful, but Ingratitude
is detestable.*

Mr. Henry Archer, a watchmaker in Morocco, had once two whelps given him, which had been stolen not long before from a lioness, near Mount Atlas. They were a male and female, and, till the death of the latter, were kept together in the emperor's garden. At that time he had the male constantly in his bed room, till it grew as tall as a large mastiff dog, and was perfectly tame and gentle in its manners. Being about to return to England, he reluctantly gave it to a Marseilles merchant, who presented it to the French king, from whom it came as a present to our king, and for seven years afterward was kept in the tower. A person of the name of Bull, who had been a servant to Mr. Archer, went by chance with some friends to see the animals there. The beast recognized him in a moment, and by his whining voice and motions, expressive of anxiety for him to come near, fully exhibited his joy at meeting with a former friend. Bull, equally pleased, ordered the keeper to open the grate, and went in. The lion fawned upon him like a dog, licking his feet, hands, and face, and skipped and tumbled about, to the astonishment of all the spectators. When the man left the place, the animal bellowed aloud, and shook his cage with sorrow; and for a few days refused to take any nourishment whatever.

APPLICATION.

It is pleasing to see acts of kindness remembered and acknowledged, while it is exceedingly painful to find them forgotten, or only returned by ingratitude. He who is grateful, shows he would be equally kind were it in his power; he who is ungrateful, degrades himself, and does great injury to all who are needy and wretched.

XXVI. THE TRAVELLER.

The many should not be condemned for the errors of the few.

"THE Americans," says Waterton, "are a gentle and civil people. Should a traveller meet with some disgraceful scenes, he ought not on his return home to adduce a solitary instance or two as the custom of the country. In roving through the wilds of Guiana, I have sometimes seen a tree hollow at heart, shattered and leafless; but I did not, on that account, condemn its vigorous neighbours, and say that the woods were bad; on the contrary, I made allowances; a thunder storm, a whirlwind, a blight from heaven, might have robbed it of its bloom, and caused its present forbidding appearance. And in leaving the forest, I carried away the impression, that though some few of the trees were defective, the rest were an ornament to the wilds, full of uses and virtues, and capable of benefiting the world in a superior degree."

APPLICATION.

"I don't like those children;" "I don't like
that school;" "I don't like the people of that
village or town!" And why not? O, it is because of one or two you think disagreeable,
and so you condemn all for them, about whom
you may, notwithstanding, be wrong. How
unfairly, how unjustly, then, do you judge!
Beside, among those you do not know, are
many with whom you would be delighted, and
who would be glad to make you happy. Far
better is it to think kindly of all, than harshly
of any one. When a little girl was asked,
"How is it that every body loves you?" she
replied, "I don't know, except it is because
I love every body."

———

XXVII. THE BEDOUIN.

*Prejudice against persons or things should be
avoided.*

"When at Alexandria," says M. Acerbi,
"I had one day ordered the two giraffes, taken
at Darfûr, to be led up and down the square
in front of my house; among the crowd collected on the occasion were some Bedouins
of the desert. On inquiring of one of them
whether he had ever seen similar animals before, he replied that he had not; and I then
asked him in Arabic, '*Taib di?*' 'Do they
please you?' To which he rejoined, '*Mustaib,*'
or, 'I do not like them.' Having desired of

my interpreter to inquire the motives of his disapproval, he answered, that the giraffe did not carry like a horse, did not serve for field labours like an ox, did not yield hair like a camel, nor flesh and milk like a goat; and on this account it was not to his liking."

APPLICATION.

The Arab was wrong in one respect; for it is a narrow view of Providence, and perhaps a selfish one, to limit our notions of the use of any being in the wide field of creation by a reference to its ability to benefit ourselves. That all creatures advance some wise purpose in the arrangement of the world is evident, from the care which has been observed to provide every species with the means for its preservation. Those which are few in number, such as the giraffe, have the means of obtaining food in a peculiar manner; live in solitary districts where the want of pasture neither brings the herd nor their destroyers; and have great quickness of sight and hearing, and the ability of rapid flight. Among the peculiarities by which the giraffe is enabled to secure his race from the attacks of the stronger, is the construction of his eye, by which he can see his enemy on every side. The Arab, however, did well if he were accustomed to judge of the value of things by their utility; that which is of great use, though unsightly, is very valuable; that which is of *no use*, is worthless.

XXVIII. THE KING OF THE VULTURES

Superiors should be attended to before us.

THE king of the vultures is very handsome, and seems to be the only bird which claims kingly honours from a surrounding tribe. It is a fact beyond all dispute, that when the scent of carrion has drawn together hundreds of the common vultures, they all retire from the carcass as soon as the monarch makes his appearance. When his majesty has satisfied the cravings of his stomach with the choicest bits, he generally retires to a neighbouring tree, and then the common vultures return in crowds to devour what he has left.

APPLICATION.

" I want some meat,"—" Give me a piece of pie,"—says an ill-behaved boy or girl, as soon as these things come on the table, and before others are helped. Why do they not sit still, and let their plate lie where it was placed, till they can be attended to? Rude children! the vultures might teach you better manners.

XXIX. THE ORCHIS.

That which is thought wrong may yet be right.

A GENTLEMAN stated some years ago, that a species of orchis is found in the hilly parts of Kent, which has in it *the form of a bee*, apparently feeding on the breast of the flower ;

and so exact is the resemblance said to be, that it is called the bee flower, and at a very small distance, it is impossible to detect the imposition.

A friend of his, however, who saw this account, wrote to him, saying—" The orchis is found near our sea coasts, but instead of being exactly like a bee, *it is not like one at all.* It has indeed a general resemblance to a fly, and, by the help of imagination, may be supposed to be a fly perched upon the flower. The mandrake very frequently has a forked root, which may be fancied to resemble thighs and legs; and I have seen it helped out with nails on the toes."

Now, which of these persons was right? It seems one must be wrong; which of them then shall we disbelieve? *Neither! Both* are right! The fact is, there are two kinds of orchis: the *bee* orchis, and the *fly* orchis. Thus there was an error on the part of the writer last mentioned; for he should not have asserted that the representation on the flower was that of a fly, till he was quite certain that there was not one with the figure of a bee.

APPLICATION.

Be very cautious in all you say;—never be too positive;—you will often be wrong when you feel sure of being right. And then never condemn hastily what others say. They may after all be right, though you at first feel certain they are wrong. It is quite possible,

you see, for two different and opposing state-
ments to be true. It is said that two knights
quarrelled, fought, and wounded each other
about a shield that stood between them; the
one said it was red, the other said it was blue:
but at length some one interfered, and showed
that it had a red side and a blue side; that each
of them therefore was right; and that had they
been wiser, and looked *at both sides*, the strife
would have been prevented.

XXX. THE THRUSHES.

*All, but especially the suffering, should be
treated kindly.*

WE observed, says a naturalist, this summer, two common thrushes frequenting the
shrubs on the green in our garden. From
the slenderness of their forms, and the freshness of their plumage, we pronounced them
to be birds of the preceding summer. A friendship appeared between them, which called our
attention to their actions : one of them seemed ailing or feeble, from some bodily accident;
for though it hopped about, yet it appeared
unable to obtain a sufficiency of food; its companion, an active sprightly bird, would generally bring it worms or bruised snails, when
they mutually partook of the provision; and
the ailing bird would wait patiently, under-
stand the actions, expect the assistance of

the other, and advance from his asylum at his approach. This procedure was continued some days, but after a time we missed the fostered bird, which probably died, or by reason of its weakness met with some fatal accident.

APPLICATION.

Unkindness is often reproved by inferior creatures. How disgraceful, then, is it to a man, a woman, a child; and what is more, how sinful! Surely we ought to be as superior *in conduct* to the birds of the air and the beasts of the field, as we are *in the favours* which God has given us. Particularly should kindness be cherished between brothers and sisters. Cato the younger, when a child, was asked one day, " Whom he loved most?" He answered, " My brother." The inquirer then asked him, " Whom he loved next?" and again he said, " My brother." " Whom in the third place?" and the reply was still, " My brother!" Have you a brother or a sister ill? Imitate the little bird of whom you have been reading, and do all you can to relieve the sufferer. Think every attention not a toil but a pleasure. The reward of kindness is sure!

XXXI. THE CRIMEA.

Flattery injures the flatterer.

ABOUT thirty years ago, many persons greatly praised one part of the empress of Russia's dominions. Among these was an eminent man, who afterward suffered from his own too favourable representations. Having published a work in which he described the Crimea as an earthly paradise, the empress sent him to reside there, on an estate which she gave him. "There," says Dr. Clarke, "we found him, as he himself confessed, in a pestilential air, the dupe of the sacrifice he had made to gratify his sovereign."

APPLICATION.

Never withhold praise from any one to whom it is due. To find fault where there is no occasion, is the mark of a low and degraded mind. An ingenuous and kind disposition will always be gratified by yielding just commendation. Guard too, against flattery; it is always stained with falsehood, and may bring you into many difficulties. Neither believe those who load you with praise. "He who praises you more than he was wont to do," says the Italians, "hath either deceived you, or is about to do it." And Solomon, to show that extravagant public professions are always to be suspected, has given us the proverb: "He that blesseth his friend with a loud voice, rising early in the morning, it shall be counted a curse to him."

XXXII. THE SECRETARY FALCON.

An innocent act may be thought vicious.

THERE is a bird called by the Dutch the secretary falcon, on account of a bunch of quills behind its head; for in 'Holland, clerks, when interrupted in their writing, stick their pen in their hair, behind their right ear; and to this the tuft of the bird was thought to bear some resemblance. Of this bird two different opinions have been formed. One naturalist thought it a *vain* bird; for, says he, when a painter was employed in drawing one of the secretary falcons, it approached him, looked attentively at his paper, stretched out its neck, and erected the feathers of its head, *as if admiring its own figure.* Others, however, who have observed it more closely, think differently, and are satisfied that the stretching out of its head, and the raising of its crest, take place from nothing more than the love which almost all domesticated birds evince of *having their heads scratched.* Thus the secretary falcon, when rendered familiar, is now well known to approach every person that comes near, and to stretch out its neck by way of making known this desire.

APPLICATION.

Those err who judge only from appearances. An act may *seem* right, and yet be *wrong;* as a child may appear very kind to others, when it is only because he knows that he shall have back far more than he gives.

His conduct is only praiseworthy as it is truly benevolent. And then an act which *seems* wrong may be right : as the little boy who was not at school one afternoon, was said by a companion to be a truant, when he only stayed at·home because his father had something for him to do.

XXXIII. THE FORAGERS.

Do unto others as you would they should do unto you.

DURING the war in Spain, some years ago, a captain went out with his troop on a foraging party, and they soon came to a house, the door of which was opened by a venerable man with a long white beard. On their demanding provision, he led them from the house, and on their coming to a fine field of barley, the captain wished to stop there and gather the crop. To this, however, he objected ; and as they followed him, they arrived shortly after at another field, of which he told them freely to partake. "But this crop," said the captain, " is not so good as the other ; I suppose that was your own, and this is your neighbour's ?" " No !" replied the aged man, " the other was my neighbour's, *this* is mine ! *That* I could not give you, to this you are welcome."

APPLICATION.

Who is not delighted as he beholds one who loved his neighbour as himself ? And yet he who does not, breaks a great commandment of God! He who wants others to help him, has no claim on their aid, unless he is willing in the same way, and to the same extent, to help them. The first founders of the empire of the Incas in Peru wisely taught it as one of their first rules, that men should neither say nor do any thing to others which they were unwilling others should say or do to them. When you want a favour of another, therefore, ask if you were in his place, would you be disposed to grant it; and if you would, you may prefer your request; but if not, let the want of it teach you for the future to be more kind, affectionate, and generous.

XXXIV. TUPEE AND KORRO-KORRO.

Sincerity should be cherished, and hypocrisy abhorred.

THE most respectable chiefs of New Zealand are often not to be trusted on their most solemn affirmation; and in speaking of each other in particular, they are accustomed to indulge in the wildest excesses of falsehood and slander. Yet the very persons who deal thus freely in mutual censures and misrepresentations behind each other's backs, are, face to face, the best friends imaginable. On one occasion, two chiefs, Tupee and Korro-Korro, having met on the deck of the ship *Active*, the former touched noses (the common mode of salutation) with the latter with the greatest show of cordiality, and nothing could seemingly be more sincere than the pleasure he professed at seeing his dear friend. But no sooner had Korro-Korro taken his departure, than his brother chief began to traduce him with the greatest virulence, painting his whole character in the blackest colours, and relating every story he could think of or invent to his discredit.

APPLICATION.

Hypocrisy and duplicity are unhappily not confined to savages. Often do they appear among the civilized, and even in the highest classes of society. But every where they are disgraceful and sinful. Guard then against the slightest approach to them. Never say of any one who is absent, what you would either be afraid or ashamed to say if he were present. " He of whom you delight to speak evil," says a French moralist, " may hear of it and become your enemy ; or if he do not, you will have to reproach yourself with the meanness of attacking one who had no opportunity of defending himself. If scandal is to be secret, it is the crime of a coward ; if it is to be known it is the crime of a madman." Never listen to those who deal in scandal; " he who slanders one to you, will slander you to another." Tale hearers make tale bearers ; and hence Dr. South said, " The tale hearer and the tale bearer should be hanged together—the one by the ear and the other by the tongue."

XXXV. THE MACAW.

Jealousy is disgraceful.

THE Brazilian green macaw is exceeding. ly jealous. It becomes enraged at seeing a young child sharing its mistress's caresses and favours, and tries to dart at the infant; but as its flight is short and laborious, it can only exhibit its displeasure by gestures and rest-less movements, and continues to be torment-ed by these fits till she leaves the child and takes the bird on her finger. It is then over. joyed, murmurs satisfaction, and sometimes makes a noise exactly like the laugh of an aged person. Nor can it bear the company of other parrots ; and if one be lodged in the same room, it seems to enjoy no comfort.

APPLICATION.

Who can really like such a selfish and jea-lous creature? How forbidding are its ill-natured looks and movements! Even its laugh must be disagreeable. And yet many a child likes to keep all it gets, without shar-ing it even with its brothers and sisters; it is out of temper when they are noticed, and pleased when they are passed by, or in dis-grace. How then can we love you, little boy, or you, little girl? You are far worse than the macaw.

XXXVI. THE ASSES OF THE ALPS.

"Let thine eyes look right on, and let thine eyelids look straight before thee."

THE manner in which asses descend the precipices of the Alps or the Andes is truly extraordinary. In the passes of these mountains there are often, on the one side, lofty eminences, and on the other, frightful abysses; and as these generally follow the direction of the mountain, the road, instead of lying on a level, forms, at every little distance, steep declivities of several hundred yards downward. These can only be descended by asses; and the animals themselves seem sensible of the danger by the caution which they use. When they come to the edge of one of the descents, they stop of themselves, without being checked by the rider; and if he inadvertently attempts to spur them on, they continue immovable. They seem all this time ruminating on the peril that lies before them, and preparing themselves for the encounter. They not only attentively view the road, but tremble and snort at the danger. Having prepared for their descent, they place their fore feet in a posture as if they were stopping themselves; they then also put their hinder feet together, but a little forward, as if they were about to lie down. In this attitude, having taken a survey of the road, they slide down with the swiftness of a meteor. In the meantime, all that the rider has to do is, to

keep himself fast in the saddle without check-
ing the rein ; for the least motion is sufficient
to disorder the equilibrium of the ass, in
which case both must unavoidably perish.
But their address in this rapid descent is
truly wonderful ; for in their swiftest motion,
when they seem to have lost all government
of themselves, they follow exactly the different windings of the road, as if they had pre-
viously settled in their minds the route they
were to follow, and taken every precaution
for their safety. In this journey the natives,
who are placed along the sides of the mountains, and hold themselves by the roots of
the trees, animate the beasts with shouts, and
encourage them to perseverance. Some
asses, after being long used to these journeys, acquire a kind of reputation for their
safety and skill ; and their value rises in
proportion to their fame.

APPLICATION.

" He who thinks twice," says Zeno, "before
he speaks once, will speak twice the better
for it :" and it is equally true, that he only will
act wisely, who first thinks wisely. Many
are fool hardy; they run into danger heed-
lessly and unnecessarily, and hence they
often suffer serious injury, and in some cases
the loss of life. The asses of the Alps are
far wiser than they ; *they look well before
them ;* they are always very cautious ; and
thus they escape the dangers to which they are
exposed, and are of great service to many.

XXXVII. THE CAMEL.

Anger is rarely wise.

CAMELS are eager to express their resentment, but they no longer retain any rancour when once they are satisfied; and it is even sufficient for them to believe that they have taken their vengeance. Accordingly, when an Arab has excited a camel's rage, he throws down his garments in some place near which the animal has to pass, and disposes them in such a manner, that they appear to cover a man sleeping under them. The animal recognizes the clothes, seizes them in his teeth, shakes them with violence, and tramples on them in a rage. When his anger is appeased, he leaves them, and then the owner of the garments may make his appearance, and without any fear load and guide him as he pleases.

APPLICATION.

How foolish the rage of the camel seems! and yet anger in human beings is still more so. It was a maxim given by one of the seven sages of Greece, "Be master of thine anger." Athenodorus, the philosopher, begged, on account of his age, to retire from the court of Augustus. The emperor having granted his request, the sage took leave of him with this charge: "Remember, Cesar, whenever you are angry, that you neither say nor do any thing, before you have repeated to yourself the twenty-four letters of the alphabet." Upon this, Cesar, catching him by the hand, said, "I still have need of your presence;" and he kept him a year longer. A greater, however, than he, has given the command: "Be ye angry and sin not; let not the sun go down upon your wrath." "I must not be an enemy," says a good writer, "nor would I have one. To be an enemy is sin, to have one is sorrow." Happy is he who is like Cranmer: his meekness was such, that those who did him an injury were almost sure of receiving some favour.

XXXVIII. OBERLIN.

Contentment should be sought and cherished.

OBERLIN was a good man, and a great benefactor to his country. At one time his lodging was a little garret up three pair of stairs. On a friend opening the door, the first object that caught his attention was a small bed, standing in one corner of the room, covered with hangings of brown paper. Approaching it, he found Oberlin on it, suffering greatly from a violent toothache. He rallied him about the simplicity of his curtains, and the homeliness of his apartment. "And pray," continued he, "what is the use of that little iron pan that hangs over your table?" "That is my kitchen," replied Oberlin: "I am in the habit of dining at home every day, with my parents, and they give me a large piece of bread to bring back in my pocket. At eight o'clock in the evening I put my bread into that pan, and having sprinkled it with salt, and poured a little water upon it, I place it over my lamp, and go on with my studies till ten or eleven, when I begin to feel hungry, and relish my self-cooked supper more than the greatest dainties."

APPLICATION.

What a striking instance of contentment!

" Hail, blest estate of lowliness !
Happy enjoyments of such minds,
As, rich in pure contentedness,
Can, like the reeds in roughest winds,
By yielding, make that blow but small,
By which proud oaks and cedars fall !"

And yet this is rare. Many, indeed, who have it not think it is theirs. A gentleman, it is said, had a board put up on a part of his land, on which was written—" I will give this field to any one who is really contented:" and when an applicant came he always said, " Are you contented?" The general reply was, " I am;" " Then," rejoined the gentleman, " what do you want with my field?" Thus their error was obvious. He only is really contented who is truly pious, and " godliness with contentment is great gain!" —" The highest point outward things can bring us to," says Sir Philip Sydney, " is the contentment of the mind, with which no estate can be poor, without which all estates will be miserable."

XXXIX. THE BULLFINCH.

It is only a good example that deserves imitation.

" I KNOW a curious person," says a writer, " who having whistled some airs quite plain to a bullfinch, was agreeably surprised to hear the bird add such graceful turns, that the master could scarcely recognize his own music, and acknowledged that the scholar excelled him." If, however, the bullfinch be ill-directed, it acquires harsh strains. A friend of the Conte de Buffon saw one that had never heard any one whistle but carters, and it whistled like them, with the same strength and coarseness.

APPLICATION.

Children like to say what others say, and to do what others do. Unhappily, however, they often imitate the ignorant rather than the intelligent—the low and vulgar rather than the well-bred. Now this is wrong—those who speak *well* and do *well* should alone be imitated.

XL. THE PINNA AND ITS CANCER FRIEND.

A little aid may often be of great service.

THERE is a large kind of muscle, called the pinna; it has a voracious enemy in the cuttle fish, which has eight long arms; and whenever the pinna opens its shell to take in its

food, the cuttle fish is on the watch to thrust
in its long arms and devour it. But it is so
ordered by Providence, that a little crab,
which has red eyes and sees very sharply,
lives in the muscle's shell, and whenever his
blind friend opens it, the crab looks out for
the enemy ; and as soon as he sees him coming, he tells the muscle, by giving him a little
pinch with his claw, and so he immediately
closes the shell, as a man fastens up his
house and shuts out the thieves.

APPLICATION.

"Two," says Solomon, "are better than
one ; for if one fall, he can help the other ;
but wo unto him who is alone when he fall-
eth." The cobbler could not paint the picture, but he could tell Apelles that the shoe
latchet was not quite right and the painter
thought it well to take his hint. Two neighbours, one blind and the other lame, were
called to a place at a great distance. What
was to be done? The blind man could not
see, and the lame man could not walk!
Why, the blind man carried the lame one ;
the former assisting by his legs, and the other
by his eyes. Say to no one then, " I can do
without you ;" but be ready to help those who
ask your aid, and then, when it is needed,
you may ask theirs. " Mankind are so much
indebted to each other," says Duclos, " that
they owe mutual attention."

XLI. THE WOODPECKER.

Truth is always precious.

On the banks of the Demerara there are
fourteen species of the woodpecker—the largest the size of a magpie, the smallest no big-
ger than the wren.   They are all beautiful;
and the greater part of them have their heads
ornamented with a fine crest, movable at
pleasure.   The sound which the largest kind
makes in hammering against the bark of a
tree is so loud, that you would never suppose
it to proceed from the efforts of a bird.   You
would take it to be the woodman, with his axe,
trying by a sturdy blow, often repeated, whether the tree were sound or not.   " The woodpecker," says Waterton, " has long laboured
under reproach.   The proprietors of woods
in Europe have long accused him of injuring
their timber, by boring holes in it, and letting in
the water, which soon rots it.   The colonists in
America have the same complaint against him.
Had he the power of speech, which Ovid's birds
possessed in days of yore, he would soon
make a defence.   ' Mighty lord of the woods,'
he would say to man, ' why do you wrong-
fully accuse me ? Why do you hunt me up
and down to death for an imaginary offence ?
I have never spoiled a leaf of your property,
much less your wood.   Your merciless shot
strikes me at the very time I am doing you a
service : but your short sightedness will not

6

let you see it, or your pride is above examining closely the actions of so insignificant a little bird as I am. If there be that spark of feeling in your breast, which they say man possesses, or ought to possess, above all other animals, do a poor injured creature a little kindness, and watch me only for one day. I never wound your healthy trees. I should perish for want in the attempt. The sound bark would easily resist the force of my bill; and were I even to pierce through it, there would be nothing inside that I could fancy, or my stomach digest. I often visit them, it is true; but a knock or two convinces me that I must go elsewhere for support; and were you to listen attentively to the sound which my bill causes, you would know whether I am upon a healthy or unhealthy tree. Wood and bark are not my food: I live entirely upon the insects which have already formed a lodgment in the distempered tree. When the sound informs me that my prey is there, I labour for hours together till I get at it; and by consuming it for my own support, I prevent its farther depredations in that part. Thus I discover for you your hidden and unsuspected foe, which has been devouring your wood in such secrecy, that you had not the least suspicion it was there. The hole which I make, in order to get at the pernicious vermin, will be seen by you as you pass under the tree. I leave it as a signal to tell you, that your tree has already stood too long. It is past its prime. Millions of insects, engendered by disease, are preying upon its vitals. Ere long it will fall a log in useless ruins. Warned by this loss, cut down the rest in time; and spare, O spare, the unoffending woodpecker!'"

APPLICATION.

"Love those who advise you," says Boileau, "not those who praise you." And yet, perhaps, whenever a relative or friend tells you what you should know or do, or how you should correct what is wrong, you think him very harsh, and cross, and unkind. Think him so then no longer. Whatever is kindly meant should always be kindly taken; and even when what is true and useful is said unkindly it ought to be received. It is well to learn of an enemy. And there is one little verse which you can commit to memory before you read farther:—

"Seize then on truth where'er 'tis found,
    Among your friends, among your foes;
On Christian or on heathen ground,
    The plant's Divine where'er it grows!"

XLII. THE ROOKS.

The sufferings of others should awaken sympathy.

"A LARGE colony of rooks," says Dr. Percival, "subsisted many years in a grove on the banks of the river Irwell, near Manchester. One serene evening I placed myself within the view of it, and marked with atten-

tion the various labours, evolutions, and pas-
times, of this crowded society. The idle
members amused themselves with chasing
each other through endless mazes; and, in
their flight, they made the air sound with a
variety of discordant noises. In the midst of
these playful exertions, it unfortunately happened that one rook by a sudden turn, struck
his beak against the wing of another. The
sufferer instantly fell into the river. A general cry of distress ensued. The birds hovered
with every expression of anxiety over their
distressed companion. Animated by their
sympathy, and, perhaps, by the language of
counsel known to themselves, he sprang into
the air, and by one strong effort, reached the
point of rock which projected into the water.
The joy became universal; but alas! it was
soon changed into notes of lamentation; for
the poor wounded bird, in attempting to fly toward his nest, dropped into the river, and was
drowned, amid the moans of his whole frater-
nity."

APPLICATION.

Children sometimes show but little feeling
and sympathy in reference to others. If, in
the midst of their games, one should be hurt,
few perhaps, if any, care for him; and if he
succeeds, instead of rejoicing with him, he is
often looked at with envy and dislike. Still
worse is it when they try to tease and annoy one
another. Should a little boy or girl have something very nice or good, some will do all they

can to snatch or spoil it ; and so far from being sorry for any who are weak and in pain, it is not uncommon for a child when unwell, to be laughed at, or mocked, or pushed, without any concern. Might not the rooks teach them better ?

XLIII. THE SPIDER, THE ANT LION, AND THE TREES.

Some see, but see not ; while the Knowledge of others is greatly increased by Observation.

It is said that a prisoner, under cruelty and injustice, shut out from society, and not permitted to have books, took an interest, and found consolation in the visits of a spider to his cell. And this is not improbable ; for the operations of that little creature are among the most extraordinary exhibitions of mechanical ingenuity, and the daily watching of the workings of its instinct is calculated to excite admiration. Bonnet, speaking of himself, says, " I knew a naturalist, who, when he was seventeen years of age, having heard of the operations of the ant lion, began by doubting them. He had no rest till he examined into them; he verified them, he admired them, he discovered new facts, and soon became the disciple and friend of the Pliny of France;"—he means the most celebrated student of nature in that country. And, says another, speaking of himself and some friends, " We made our excursion, some weeks ago, to Westwood, near Shooter's Hill, expressly for the purpose of observing the insects we might meet with in the wood; but we had not got far among the bushes, before heavy rain came on. We immediately sought shelter among the boughs of some thick underwood, composed of oak, birch, and aspen; but we could not meet with a single insect sheltered under the leaves. Upon looking, however, more narrowly into the bushes, we soon found a variety of interesting objects. The oak abounded in *galls*, several of them quite new to us, while the leaves of the birch and the aspen exhibited the curious serpentine paths of the minute mining caterpillars. When we had exhausted this narrow field of observation, we found we could extend it, by breaking a few of the taller branches near us, and then examining their *leaves* at leisure. In this manner two hours quickly and pleasantly glided away, by which time the rain had nearly ceased; and though we had been disappointed of our ramble through the wood, we did not return without adding a few interesting facts to our previous knowledge."

APPLICATION.

Try, at all times, to learn something. Every thing in the world of nature is not only worth *seeing*, but worth *noticing*. Many are ignorant because they see but *observe* not. In every spot we may increase our knowledge by a good use of our eyes; either by finding out what we did not know, or by gathering questions to have answered by those who know more than ourselves.

XLIV. POMAREE.

Selfishness is vexatious, painful, and ruinous.

"POMAREE, a New Zealand chief," says Mr. Nicholas, "had cast a longing eye upon a chisel belonging to one of the missionaries, and to obtain it he had brought some fish on board, which he presented to the owner of the chisel with so much apparent generosity and friendliness, that the other could not help considering it a gratuitous favour, and receiving it as such, told him he felt very grateful for his kindness. But Pomaree had no idea of any such disinterested liberality; and as soon as the fish was eaten, he immediately demanded the chisel in return, which however was not granted, as it was a present much too valuable to be given away for so trifling a consideration. Incensed at the denial, the chief flew into a violent rage, and testified, by loud reproaches, how grievously he was provoked by the ill success of his project. He told the person, who very properly refused to comply with his demand, that 'he was no good,' and that he would never again bring him any thing more. He attempted the same crafty experiment on another of our party, but this proved also equally abortive, the person being well aware of his character, and knowing that he would require of him ten times more than the worth of his pretended favour.

APPLICATION.

Selfishness should always be condemned; as, in the case of Pomaree, it often issues in disappointment. It is said, that a man had a very large turnip, and that on making a present of it to the great man of the place, he very unexpectedly received for the curiosity five hundred crowns. A neighbour, on hearing this, thought that he should obtain a much larger sum if he presented a beautiful and rare pony; but the great man, detecting his selfishness, said, "Give him the turnip, and tell him it cost me five hundred crowns." Selfishness is also painful. A greedy child may well be called a little miser, a name which shows that he to whom it is given is unhappy, as those must always be who do wrong. And then selfishness produces a variety of evils. Gluttony, falsehood, theft, are among its offspring, and by them many are disgraced and ruined.

XLV. THE WHITE OWL.

All are dependent.

JENGHIS KHAN, the founder of the empire of
the Mongol and Calmuc Tartars, happened,
with a small army, to be surprised and put to
flight by his enemies. Compelled to seek concealment in a coppice, an owl settled on the
bush beneath which he was hidden. This circumstance induced his pursuers not to search
there, supposing that that bird would not perch
where any man was concealed. The prince
therefore escaped; and thenceforth his coun-
trymen held the white owl sacred, and every
one wore a plume of its feathers on his head.

APPLICATION.

Despise no one—despise nothing. The meanest person—the meanest thing may one day be

of great service! Paper, for instance, is now manufactured very extensively by machinery, in all its stages; and thus, instead of a single sheet being made by hand, a stream of paper is poured out, which would form a roll large enough to extend round the globe, if such a length were desirable. Its inventors, it is said, spent the enormous sum of 40,000*l.* in vain attempts to render the machine capable of determining the exact length of the roll; and at last accomplished their object, at the suggestion of a by-stander, by a strap revolving on an axis, at a cost of *three shillings and six pence.*

The lowest are useful as well as the highest. If the rich benefit the poor, the poor labour for the rich. The king protects his subjects; but "the king is served by the labour of the field." There is no such thing as independence, and he who says there is, only discovers his ignorance and pride.

XLVI. THE TORTOISE AND THE ELEPHANT.

Good Feeling, though awkwardly expressed, is far better than hypocritical Courtesy.

A GREEK tortoise was in the possession of a lady in Sussex upward of thirty years. Mr. White, of Selbourne, watched it very close, and was much pleased with its sagacity in distinguishing those from whom it was accustomed to receive attention. Whenever the lady who had so long waited on it came in sight, it always hobbled, with awkward alacrity, toward its benefactress: thus did the most abject of torpid creatures distinguish the hand that fed it, and exhibit marks of gratitude not always to be found in superior orders of animal being.

Mr. Forbes had an elephant, of which he was very fond; it had carried him many a long march, and had attached him to it by its sweetness of disposition. If he wished to enjoy a prospect, he had only to speak, and the elephant remained motionless till he gave it the signal to proceed. If he had a desire for the ripe mangoes that grew on the upper branches, it advanced to that part of the tree, and, breaking off the most fruitful bough with his trunk, he offered it to the driver for the company in his houdah; and if he received any part for his trouble, he accepted it with profound respect, making a salaam, or obeisance, three times, with his trunk raised to the top of his head, and as often did he express his thanks by a murmuring noise.

APPLICATION.

All are pleased with kind feelings, even though clumsily expressed, while nothing is more offensive than the appearance of them when they are wanting. Sincerity with many blunders is better than hypocrisy with all its affected courtesy. He who feels aright may be excused if not so polished as others; he who does not, increases his fault, by his forced and pretended civilities.

XLVII. THE MUSCLES.

When one Means fails, try Another.

On the northern coast of Ireland, a friend of Dr. Darwin saw above a hundred crows at once preying upon muscles: the mode of doing this was remarkable—each crow took a muscle up in the air twenty or forty yards high, and let it fall on the stones; and thus, by breaking the shell got possession of the animal.

APPLICATION.

"I can't do it"—is often a very silly speech. One trial more and the thing perhaps may be done. But should this fail, it may be done in *another way.* The crow who could not open the shell with its beak, broke it by a fall, and so got the muscle; and the little boy or girl who is told to do any thing, should not give it up till *all ways* are tried.

———

XLVIII. THE TURKS.

There is a right Way and a wrong Way.

"The Turks differ from the Franks," says Dr. Walsh, "in their most trifling habits. The barber pushes his razor from him, ours draws it to him; the carpenter, on the contrary, drew the saw to him, for all the teeth were set in; ours pushes it from him, for all the teeth are set out: the mason sat while he laid the stones, ours always stands; the scribe wrote on his hand, and from right to left; ours always writes on a desk, and from left to right: but the most ridiculous difference consisted in the manner of building a house—we begin at the bottom and finish at the top: the house we now saw was a frame of wood, which the Turks began at the top, and the upper rooms were finished and inhabited, while all below was like a lantern."

APPLICATION.

There are two ways of doing a thing—a right way and a wrong way. Now the right way is always the easier and the more agreeable, while the wrong way is always difficult and troublesome. Beside, when a thing is done wrong, it has to be done over again. When children do not know how to do any thing in the best manner, they should inquire of their parents, teachers, or friends; and when they are told, they should remember and attend to what has been said. Many a mother has said to her little girl, " Your work is all wrong—do you not see how ill it looks? —go and pull it all out again;"—and many a little boy has had his sum rubbed out from his slate because he did not mind what was said; or, taking the wrong turning, and going down the wrong street, has not been able to find out the person to whom he has been sent, and has had to go again for his negligence and thoughtlessness.

XLIX. SNAKES AND MONKEYS.

Mischief is censurable.

"Snakes, in the wilds of Demerara," says Waterton, "are certainly an annoyance, though perhaps more in imagination than reality ; for you must recollect, that *the serpent is never the first to offend :* his poisonous fang was not given him for conquest : he never inflicts a wound with it, but to defend existence. Provided you walk cautiously, and do not absolutely touch him, you may pass in safety close by him."

In another place he remarks, " Probably travellers have erred, in asserting that the monkeys of South America throw sticks and fruit at their pursuers. I have had fine opportunities of narrowly watching the different species of monkeys which are found in the wilds, between the Amazons and the Oroonoque. I entirely acquit them of acting on the offensive. When the monkeys are in the high trees over your head, the dead branches will now and then fall down upon you, having been broken off as the Monkeys pass along them; but they are never hurled from their hands."

APPLICATION.

Some children delight in mischief. For their own sport they injure or destroy the playthings of others—put things in their way for them to fall over and hurt themselves—

or tie kettles or weights to the tails of dogs that they may have what they call fun. But this is very unamiable—it shows an unkind, and often a spiteful disposition, and makes them far worse than serpents and monkeys.

L. ABDOULRAHMAN.

The Great are not always happy.

ABDOULRAHMAN THE THIRD was the most distinguished and prosperous of all the Spanish kings of the Arabian race. He obtained many triumphs, adorned his kingdom with magnificent and useful public buildings, and had a revenue, without oppressing his people, sufficient for all his purposes. Every one pronounced him to be a happy prince. But how different was his own opinion, written by his own hand, and found in his repositories after his death: "From the time I ascended the throne, I marked every day that afforded me true pleasure, and these days amounted to *fourteen!* Mortals! consider what this world is, and how little we ought to rely upon its pleasures. Yet nothing seems wanting to my felicity ; neither riches—nor honours— nor sovereign power. Neighbouring princes envy my happiness, are jealous of my glory, and ambitious of my friendship. I have reigned fifty years, and yet in so long a time, I have not been able to count more than fourteen days free from vexation and trouble."

APPLICATION.

How common is envy—that evil passion which consists in being uneasy and unhappy at the prosperity of others. "And yet," says Dr. Young, "if we did but know how *little* some *enjoy* of the great things they possess, there would not be much envy in the world." The case of Abdoulrahman is by no means rare. Pope Adrian VI. was the son of a poor barge builder at Utrecht, but after having risen to great worldly honours, he desired the following inscription to be placed over his tomb:—"Here lies Adrian VI., who esteemed no misfortune which happened to him in life so great as his being called to govern." Envy then is foolish, but it is also prejudicial; hence it has been said to "consume the envious as rust does iron;" not unfrequently it is accompanied by malignity—than which no disposition is more base or more wicked.

THE END.